Soul Rubbing Exercises

A Personal Vision Quest

The author of this book does not dispense medical advice nor prescribe the use of the exercises and her philosophy for living as a form of treatment for physical or medical problems without the advice of a physician, either directly or indirectly. The intent of the author is only to offer information and statements that may assist you in taking responsibility for your own mental, physical, emotional and spiritual health and to assist humanity in understanding that what affects one will affect all.

In the event that you undertake these exercises, and apply the eight-point philosophy for living to your own life, the author and publisher assume no responsibility for your actions.

Cover Artwork by Daughter of Barbara J. Gill.

Printed by Lulu, www.lulu.com
Morrisville, NC, USA

Published by EVENTS PLANNING ASSOCIATES LTD. /
ASSOCIES PLANIFICATION D'EVENEMENTS LTEE.

Fredericton, NB, Canada

Library and Archives Canada Cataloguing in Publication

Gill, Barbara J., 1951-
Soul Rubbing Exercises : A Personal Vision Quest /
Barbara J.Gill ; introduction by Carol Desjarlais.

Companion book to Soul Gifts.
ISBN 978-1-4116-9045-5

1. Conduct of life. I. Gill, Barbara J., 1951- . Soul Gifts II. Title.

BJ1581.2.G538 2005a 170'.44 C2006-902495-2

Dedicated to The World's Children

8% of author profits from Soul Gifts will be donated to Doctors Without Borders/ Médecins Sans Frontières (MSF). Readers are encouraged to contribute directly to this Nobel Peace Prize-winning organization. http://www.msf.org.

Dear Reader,

Soul Rubbing Exercises: A Personal Vision Quest was developed as a companion book to *Soul Gifts: The World's Self-Help Book*. Each of the exercises deepens the personal exploration of my philosophy for living:

You.

You Can.

You Can Risk.

You Can Risk Change.

You Can Risk Change. Be Gentle.

You Can Risk Change. Be Gentle. Be Giving.

You Can Risk Change. Be Gentle. Be Giving. Grow.

You Can Risk Change. Be Gentle. Be Giving. Grow. Pass It On.

I met Carol Desjarlais in the spring of 2005. Known by some as Eagle Woman, Carol is of the Woodland Cree, Alberta, Canada and now lives in the United States. She is a Traditionalist Medicine Woman and a prolific poet. A caring, generous and vibrant healer, Carol taught in Native American educational settings and retrieved troubled youth.

For many years Carol has created artwork centered around the theme, "Woman of the Pots". Her geographical move from Canada to the US serendipitously positioned her in Maine - an hour's drive from Mike McCabe in New Hampshire. (See McCabe in Soul Gifts: The World's Self-Help Book, Chapters One, Two and Eight). In 2003 Mike introduced me to the descriptive phrase "Pot of Thoughts". It is used in each of the eight exercises.

While working through her own "Pot of Thoughts", Carol created extensive pictorial and poetry scrapbooks which she shares with family, friends and newcomers to her life. She finds this is a growing experience for herself and others. Watch for the publication of these scrapbooks in the future.

Carol named this book. Her introduction to the exercises follows on the next page.

Barbara J. Gill, R.N.
New Brunswick, Canada.
www.shandarrah.com

INTRODUCTION

If we want to give a gift, we want to give a worthy gift. These exercises give us the opportunity to take a long and soulful look at things that may seem ordinary, but at soul level, are not. It is easy to just stroke down some words to give reply to the statements, but that does not add depth and understanding. It takes long and concentrated thought to find a way to respond soulfully.

When reading the statements, consider why it is that you choose what you do. For instance, how does what you wear express something soul deep? The kinds of shoes I have worn throughout my life became the metaphor for who I was. On considering, deeply, how my smell affects others, I choose to write about fresh fried bannock and how it would smell delicious to a hungry person. I wrote how, if I smelled of fish scales that I had stripped from the fish, you would admire my art. I described how I may smell of earth and yet another would admire my peonies. If you were my child, I could smell of breast milk and you would know me.

On writing about my voice, I thought of whispering against a child's cheek, how the mew of my mouth holds in grief, how my breath gives rise and fall to the things that touch me and call me to expression, and how my voice can comfort another like a blanket.

I encourage you to begin with the first statement. Do not peek at what is coming. Doing this work has its own momentum. Allow time for the thought to settle in and brew. We are not all poetically inclined. You may do lists, but do the lists in free writing. Allow the list to become its own force. Set it aside and look back at it. Keep adding more words, phrases, sentences and memories as you continue on with developing your gift.

Everyone's soul seeks its source. I believe that the depth of our self-knowledge and our self-expression of that knowledge makes Source aware of us. We vibrate the world with our being here. The vibrations we make are ripples that eventually bounce back to us. Soul-rubbing. This is your opportunity to become aware of how you vibrate: physically, intellectually, emotionally and spiritually.

Happy soul-rubbing,
Carol Desjarlais
Bridgton, ME, US.

SOUL RUBBING ONE:

You

This exercise has been developed to give you the opportunity to consider:

(1) How you perceive yourself,

(2) How you perceive the way others perceive you,

(3) How you perceive your choices affecting others,

(4) How you perceive the impact your choices have on your body and conscious mind.

The statements following are a starting point and they are not all-encompassing. They are intended to be accomplished over weeks . . . months.

Tick off *yes*, *no* or *maybe* where applicable and elaborate your thoughts in the space provided. In other instances circle the answer that you most identify with.

1. I like the way I choose to look.

☐ Yes ☐ No ☐ Maybe

My Pot of Thoughts:____

____

____

____

2. I perceive that others like the way I choose to look.

☐ Yes ☐ No ☐ Maybe

My Pot of Thoughts:____

____

____

____

3. I like the way I choose to smell.

☐ Yes ☐ No ☐ Maybe

My Pot of Thoughts:____

____

____

____

4. I perceive that others like the way I choose to smell.

☐ Yes ☐ No ☐ Maybe

My Pot of Thoughts:____

____

____

____

5. I like the way I choose to walk.

☐ Yes ☐ No ☐ Maybe

My Pot of Thoughts:____

____

____

____

6. I perceive that others like the way I choose to walk.

☐ Yes ☐ No ☐ Maybe

My Pot of Thoughts:____

____

____

____

7. I like the way I choose to think.

☐ Yes ☐ No ☐ Maybe

My Pot of Thoughts:____

8. I perceive that others like the way I choose to think.

☐ Yes ☐ No ☐ Maybe

My Pot of Thoughts:____

9. I perceive that the way I choose to think has an impact on others.

☐ Yes ☐ No ☐ Maybe

My Pot of Thoughts:____

10. I perceive that the way I choose to think has an impact on my bodily functions.

☐ Yes ☐ No ☐ Maybe

My Pot of Thoughts:____

11. I like the sounds I choose to make with my voice.

☐ Yes ☐ No ☐ Maybe

My Pot of Thoughts:____

12. I perceive that others like the sounds I choose to make with my voice.

☐ Yes ☐ No ☐ Maybe

My Pot of Thoughts:____

13. I like what I choose to say when I speak.

☐ Yes ☐ No ☐ Maybe

My Pot of Thoughts:____

14. I perceive that others like what I choose to say when I speak.

☐ Yes ☐ No ☐ Maybe

My Pot of Thoughts:____

15. I like the *way* that I choose to eat and drink. ***(i.e. I use my fingers or utensils, eat/drink quickly or slowly, with my mouth closed or open)***

☐ Yes ☐ No ☐ Maybe

My Pot of Thoughts:______________________________

____

____

____

16. I perceive that others like the *way* I choose to eat or drink.

☐ Yes ☐ No ☐ Maybe

My Pot of Thoughts:______________________________

____

____

____

17. I perceive that my body likes the *way* I choose to eat or drink.

☐ Yes ☐ No ☐ Maybe

My Pot of Thoughts:______________________________

____

____

____

18. I like *what* I choose to eat.

☐ Yes ☐ No ☐ Maybe

My Pot of Thoughts:______________________________

____

____

____

19. I perceive that my body likes what I choose to eat.

☐ Yes ☐ No ☐ Maybe

My Pot of Thoughts:____

20. I like what I choose to drink.

☐ Yes ☐ No ☐ Maybe

My Pot of Thoughts:____

21. I perceive that my body likes what I choose to drink.

☐ Yes ☐ No ☐ Maybe

My Pot of Thoughts:____

22. I like what drugs I choose to feed my body. ***(i.e. any substance such as prescription medications, over the counter medications/natural supplements, street drugs, alcohol, cigarettes)***

☐ Yes ☐ No ☐ Maybe

My Pot of Thoughts:____

23. I perceive that the drugs I choose to feed my body have an impact on others. (Elaborate positive /negative experiences resulting from these choices.)

☐ Yes ☐ No ☐ Maybe

My Pot of Thoughts:____

____

____

____

24. I perceive that the drugs I choose to feed my body have an impact on my body. (Elaborate positive /negative experiences resulting from these choices.)

☐ Yes ☐ No ☐ Maybe

My Pot of Thoughts:____

____

____

____

25. I perceive that the drugs I choose to feed my body have an impact on my mind. (Elaborate positive /negative experiences resulting from these choices.)

☐ Yes ☐ No ☐ Maybe

My Pot of Thoughts:____

____

____

____

26. I like the way I choose to exercise my body.

☐ Yes ☐ No ☐ Maybe

My Pot of Thoughts:____

____

____

27. I perceive that my body likes the way I choose to exercise it.

☐ Yes ☐ No ☐ Maybe

My Pot of Thoughts:____________________________________

28. I like the way I choose to adorn myself. ***(i.e. clothing, jewelry, tattoos, hair pieces, makeup, body piercing etc)***

☐ Yes ☐ No ☐ Maybe

My Pot of Thoughts:____________________________________

29. I perceive that others like the way I choose to adorn myself.

☐ Yes ☐ No ☐ Maybe

My Pot of Thoughts:____________________________________

30. I perceive that my body likes the way I choose to adorn it.

☐ Yes ☐ No ☐ Maybe

My Pot of Thoughts:____________________________________

31. I perceive that my mind likes the way I choose to adorn my body.

☐ Yes ☐ No ☐ Maybe

My Pot of Thoughts:____

32. I will describe my body.

☐ Yes ☐ No ☐ Maybe

My Pot of Thoughts:____

33. I will describe how I perceive that others describe my body.

☐ Yes ☐ No ☐ Maybe

My Pot of Thoughts:____

34. I will explain how my body would perceive itself. *(i.e. what your body would tell you about itself)*

☐ Yes ☐ No ☐ Maybe

My Pot of Thoughts:____

35. I like what I choose to wear on my feet.

☐ Yes ☐ No ☐ Maybe

My Pot of Thoughts:____

36. I perceive that others like what I choose to wear on my feet.

☐ Yes ☐ No ☐ Maybe

My Pot of Thoughts:____

37. I perceive that my body likes what I choose to wear on my feet.

☐ Yes ☐ No ☐ Maybe

My Pot of Thoughts:____

38. I like the way I choose to breathe.

☐ Yes ☐ No ☐ Maybe

My Pot of Thoughts:____

39. I perceive that others like the way I choose to breathe.

☐ Yes ☐ No ☐ Maybe

My Pot of Thoughts:

40. I perceive that my mind likes the way I choose to breathe.

☐ Yes ☐ No ☐ Maybe

My Pot of Thoughts:

41. I choose to meditate/contemplate/pray.

☐ Yes ☐ No ☐ Maybe

My Pot of Thoughts:

42. My meditation/contemplation/prayer affects others.

☐ Yes ☐ No ☐ Maybe

My Pot of Thoughts:

43. My meditation/contemplation/prayer affects my body.

☐ Yes ☐ No ☐ Maybe

My Pot of Thoughts:____

44. I will describe how others would describe my mind.

☐ Yes ☐ No ☐ Maybe

My Pot of Thoughts:____

45. I will describe how my mind perceives itself. ***(i.e. What would my mind tell me about itself?)***

☐ Yes ☐ No ☐ Maybe

My Pot of Thoughts:____

46. I will describe how my body perceives my mind.

☐ Yes ☐ No ☐ Maybe

My Pot of Thoughts:____

47. I like the way I choose to sleep. (*i.e. in a chair, a bed with a poor/good mattress, on the floor, dressed in pyjamas or naked)*

☐ Yes ☐ No ☐ Maybe

My Pot of Thoughts:____________________________________

____

____

____

48. I perceive that the way I choose to sleep has an impact on others.

☐ Yes ☐ No ☐ Maybe

My Pot of Thoughts:____________________________________

____

____

____

49. I perceive that the way I choose to sleep has an impact on my mind.

☐ Yes ☐ No ☐ Maybe

My Pot of Thoughts:____________________________________

____

____

____

50. I perceive that the way I choose to sleep has an impact on my body.

☐ Yes ☐ No ☐ Maybe

My Pot of Thoughts:____________________________________

____

____

____

51. I like what I choose to cast my eyes upon.

☐ Yes ☐ No ☐ Maybe

My Pot of Thoughts:____

52. I perceive that others are affected by what I choose to cast my eyes upon.

☐ Yes ☐ No ☐ Maybe

My Pot of Thoughts:____

53. I perceive that my body is affected by what I choose to cast my eyes upon.

☐ Yes ☐ No ☐ Maybe

My Pot of Thoughts:____

54. I perceive that my mind is affected by what I choose to cast my eyes upon.

☐ Yes ☐ No ☐ Maybe

My Pot of Thoughts:____

55. I like what I choose to listen to.

☐ Yes ☐ No ☐ Maybe

My Pot of Thoughts:____

56. I perceive that others are affected by what I choose to listen to.

☐ Yes ☐ No ☐ Maybe

My Pot of Thoughts:____

57. I perceive that my body is affected by what I choose to listen to.

☐ Yes ☐ No ☐ Maybe

My Pot of Thoughts:____

58. I perceive that my mind is affected by what I choose to listen to.

☐ Yes ☐ No ☐ Maybe

My Pot of Thoughts:____

59. I have sexual intimacy with another/others or with myself. (i.e. masturbation).

☐ Yes ☐ No ☐ Maybe

My Pot of Thoughts:____

____

____

____

60. I have: (Circle one)

a. No sexual partner

b. A single sexual partner

c. Multiple sexual partners

My Pot of Thoughts:____

____

____

____

61. I perceive that my body is affected by my choices regarding sexual intimacy.

☐ Yes ☐ No ☐ Maybe

My Pot of Thoughts:____

____

____

____

62. I perceive that my mind is affected by my choices regarding sexual intimacy.

☐ Yes ☐ No ☐ Maybe

My Pot of Thoughts:____________________________

63. I choose to have a good relationship with others.

☐ Yes ☐ No ☐ Maybe

My Pot of Thoughts:____________________________

64. Others perceive that I have close friends.

☐ Yes ☐ No ☐ Maybe

My Pot of Thoughts:____________________________

65. My relationship with others has an impact on my body.

☐ Yes ☐ No ☐ Maybe

My Pot of Thoughts:____________________________

66. My relationship with friends has an impact on my mind.

☐ Yes ☐ No ☐ Maybe

My Pot of Thoughts:____

67. I have a good relationship with family.

☐ Yes ☐ No ☐ Maybe

My Pot of Thoughts:____

68. Others perceive that I choose to have a good relationship with family.

☐ Yes ☐ No ☐ Maybe

My Pot of Thoughts:____

69. My relationship with family has an impact on my body.

☐ Yes ☐ No ☐ Maybe

My Pot of Thoughts:____

70. My relationship with family has an impact on my mind.

☐ Yes ☐ No ☐ Maybe

My Pot of Thoughts:

71. I like what I choose to read.

☐ Yes ☐ No ☐ Maybe

My Pot of Thoughts:

72. I perceive that what I choose to read has an impact on others.

☐ Yes ☐ No ☐ Maybe

My Pot of Thoughts:

73. I perceive that what I choose to read has an impact on my body.

☐ Yes ☐ No ☐ Maybe

My Pot of Thoughts:

74. I perceive that what I choose to read has an impact on my mind.

☐ Yes ☐ No ☐ Maybe

My Pot of Thoughts:____

75. I choose to work. (The term work includes time spent as a paid employee, a stay at home mum/caregiver etc., a volunteer)

☐ Yes ☐ No ☐ Maybe

My Pot of Thoughts:____

76. Others perceive that I choose to work.

☐ Yes ☐ No ☐ Maybe

My Pot of Thoughts:____

77. My work has an impact on my body.

☐ Yes ☐ No ☐ Maybe

My Pot of Thoughts:____

78. I perceive that my choice of work has an impact on my mind.

☐ Yes ☐ No ☐ Maybe

My Pot of Thoughts:____

____

____

____

79. I always choose to have an uncluttered, aesthetically pleasing and ergonomically correct physical environment.

☐ Yes ☐ No ☐ Maybe

My Pot of Thoughts:____

____

____

____

80. Others perceive that my environment is uncluttered, aesthetic and ergonomic.

☐ Yes ☐ No ☐ Maybe

My Pot of Thoughts:____

____

____

____

81. Everything I do reflects my soul's calling.

☐ Yes ☐ No ☐ Maybe

My Pot of Thoughts:____

____

____

____

82. I laugh *(circle one)*

a. A lot
b. A little
c. Sometimes
d. Never

83. I cry *(circle one)*

a. A lot
b. A little
c. Sometimes
d. Never

84. I am angry *(circle one)*

a. A lot
b. A little
c. Sometimes
d. Never

85. I will explain how I choose to express love.

☐ Yes ☐ No ☐ Maybe

My Pot of Thoughts:____

____

____

____

86. I perceive that others like the way I choose to express love.

☐ Yes ☐ No ☐ Maybe

My Pot of Thoughts:____

____

____

____

87. I perceive that my body enjoys the way I choose to express love.

☐ Yes ☐ No ☐ Maybe

My Pot of Thoughts:____

88. I perceive that my mind enjoys the way I choose to express love.

☐ Yes ☐ No ☐ Maybe

My Pot of Thoughts:____

89. I will explain how I express anger.

☐ Yes ☐ No ☐ Maybe

My Pot of Thoughts:____

90. I perceive that others enjoy the way I choose to express anger.

☐ Yes ☐ No ☐ Maybe

My Pot of Thoughts:____

91. I perceive that my body enjoys the way I choose to express anger.

☐ Yes ☐ No ☐ Maybe

My Pot of Thoughts:

92. I perceive that my mind enjoys the way I choose to express anger.

☐ Yes ☐ No ☐ Maybe

My Pot of Thoughts:

93. I have a dream/aspiration that is a secret.

☐ Yes ☐ No ☐ Maybe

My Pot of Thoughts:

94. I would like to make my dream/aspiration come true.

☐ Yes ☐ No ☐ Maybe

My Pot of Thoughts:

95. I will explain what gifts I was given when I was created/conceived.

☐ Yes ☐ No ☐ Maybe

My Pot of Thoughts:____

____

____

____

96. I will explain how I choose to use my special gifts.

☐ Yes ☐ No ☐ Maybe

My Pot of Thoughts:____

____

____

____

97. I most often choose to say no *(circle one)*

a. Loudly
b. Softly
c. Assertively
d. Defiantly

98. I perceive that my ability (or lack thereof) to say no has an impact on others.

☐ Yes ☐ No ☐ Maybe

My Pot of Thoughts:____

____

____

____

____

____

99. I perceive my ability (or lack thereof) to say no has an impact on my body.

☐ Yes ☐ No ☐ Maybe

My Pot of Thoughts:____

100. I perceive my ability (or lack thereof) to say no has an impact on my mind.

☐ Yes ☐ No ☐ Maybe

My Pot of Thoughts:____

101. I most often choose to say yes (*circle one*)

a. Loudly
b. Softly
c. Begrudgingly
d. Joyously

102. I perceive that my ability (or lack thereof) to say yes has an impact on others.

☐ Yes ☐ No ☐ Maybe

My Pot of Thoughts:____

103. I perceive my ability (or lack thereof) to say yes has an impact on my body.

☐ Yes ☐ No ☐ Maybe

My Pot of Thoughts:____

____

____

____

104. I perceive my ability (or lack thereof) to say yes has an impact on my mind.

☐ Yes ☐ No ☐ Maybe

My Pot of Thoughts:____

____

____

____

105. I like my teeth.

☐ Yes ☐ No ☐ Maybe

My Pot of Thoughts:____

____

____

____

106. I like my skin.

☐ Yes ☐ No ☐ Maybe

My Pot of Thoughts:____

____

____

____

107. I like my hair.

☐ Yes ☐ No ☐ Maybe

My Pot of Thoughts:____

108. I like my legs.

☐ Yes ☐ No ☐ Maybe

My Pot of Thoughts:____

109. I like my arms.

☐ Yes ☐ No ☐ Maybe

My Pot of Thoughts:____

110. I like my ears.

☐ Yes ☐ No ☐ Maybe

My Pot of Thoughts:____

111. I like my eyes.

☐ Yes ☐ No ☐ Maybe

My Pot of Thoughts:____

112. I like my fingers.

☐ Yes ☐ No ☐ Maybe

My Pot of Thoughts:____

113. I like my toes.

☐ Yes ☐ No ☐ Maybe

My Pot of Thoughts:____

114. I like my breasts.

☐ Yes ☐ No ☐ Maybe

My Pot of Thoughts:____

115. I like my genitals.

☐ Yes ☐ No ☐ Maybe

My Pot of Thoughts:____

116. I have difficulty with bodily functions such as urination, bowel movements, sexual arousal, breathing, swallowing, sweating etc. Elaborate.

☐ Yes ☐ No ☐ Maybe

My Pot of Thoughts:____

117. I have cravings and choose to give into them.

☐ Yes ☐ No ☐ Maybe

My Pot of Thoughts:____

118. I perceive that others are affected by my cravings.

☐ Yes ☐ No ☐ Maybe

My Pot of Thoughts:____

119. I perceive that my body is affected by my cravings.

☐ Yes ☐ No ☐ Maybe

My Pot of Thoughts:____

120. I perceive that my mind is affected by my cravings.

☐ Yes ☐ No ☐ Maybe

My Pot of Thoughts:____

121. I have yearnings.

☐ Yes ☐ No ☐ Maybe

My Pot of Thoughts:____

122. I perceive that others are affected by my yearnings.

☐ Yes ☐ No ☐ Maybe

My Pot of Thoughts:____

123. I perceive that my body is affected by my yearnings.

☐ Yes ☐ No ☐ Maybe

My Pot of Thoughts:

124. I perceive that my mind is affected by my yearnings.

☐ Yes ☐ No ☐ Maybe

My Pot of Thoughts:

125. I consider myself intelligent.

☐ Yes ☐ No ☐ Maybe

My Pot of Thoughts:

126. I perceive that others think of me as intelligent.

☐ Yes ☐ No ☐ Maybe

My Pot of Thoughts:

127. I perceive that I make intelligent choices.

☐ Yes ☐ No ☐ Maybe

My Pot of Thoughts:____

128. I perceive that others regard my choices as intelligent.

☐ Yes ☐ No ☐ Maybe

My Pot of Thoughts:____

129. I respect myself.

☐ Yes ☐ No ☐ Maybe

My Pot of Thoughts:____

130. I perceive that others respect me.

☐ Yes ☐ No ☐ Maybe

My Pot of Thoughts:____

131. I perceive that my respect for myself (or lack thereof) has an impact on my body.

☐ Yes ☐ No ☐ Maybe

My Pot of Thoughts:____

132. I perceive that my respect for myself (or lack thereof) has an impact on my mind.

☐ Yes ☐ No ☐ Maybe

My Pot of Thoughts:____

133. I love myself.

☐ Yes ☐ No ☐ Maybe

My Pot of Thoughts:____

134. I perceive that others love me.

☐ Yes ☐ No ☐ Maybe

My Pot of Thoughts:____

135. How others perceive me is (check one)

☐ **Very important** ☐ **Somewhat important** ☐ **Not important**

My Pot of Thoughts:____

____

____

____

136. I find myself judging the actions, words or physical appearance of others. (If yes, explain why you choose to judge others.)

☐ Yes ☐ No ☐ Maybe

My Pot of Thoughts:____

____

____

____

137. I believe everybody has the right to live life as they see fit.

☐ Yes ☐ No ☐ Maybe

My Pot of Thoughts:____

____

____

____

138. I believe in law and order. (Explain your concept of law and order and why your concept should be adopted by all who inhabit Earth.)

☐ Yes ☐ No ☐ Maybe

My Pot of Thoughts:____

____

____

____

139. I know what organs are in my body, how they work and the body systems that keep the body alive.

☐ Yes ☐ No ☐ Maybe

My Pot of Thoughts:____

140. I am willing to understand the anatomy and physiology of the body and relate my discoveries to my general state of health.

☐ Yes ☐ No ☐ Maybe

My Pot of Thoughts:____

141. I will explain how much I love Earth and how I daily take steps to preserve the Planet.

☐ Yes ☐ No ☐ Maybe

My Pot of Thoughts:____

142. I will explain the relationship between my mind and body.

☐ Yes ☐ No ☐ Maybe

My Pot of Thoughts:____

143. I will explain my mind and body connection to my soul.

☐ Yes ☐ No ☐ Maybe

My Pot of Thoughts:

I have other statements to make. They are as follows:

SOUL RUBBING TWO:

You.

You Can.

PART A

Join the exciting journey into the world of the can-do attitude. List things you can do. Begin with the simple things, then work your way up to the more challenging.

Example:

- I can brush my teeth
- I can talk
- I can breathe
- I can walk
- I can wink

1. ______
2. ______
3. ______
4. ______
5. ______
6. ______
7. ______
8. ______
9. ______
10. ______
11. ______
12. ______
13. ______
14. ______
15. ______
16. ______
17. ______
18. ______
19. ______
20. ______
21. ______
22. ______
23. ______
24. ______
25. ______
26. ______
27. ______
28. ______
29. ______
30. ______

31. ____________________
32. ____________________
33. ____________________
34. ____________________
35. ____________________
36. ____________________
37. ____________________
38. ____________________
39. ____________________
40. ____________________
41. ____________________
42. ____________________
43. ____________________
44. ____________________
45. ____________________
46. ____________________
47. ____________________
48. ____________________
49. ____________________
50. ____________________
51. ____________________
52. ____________________
53. ____________________
54. ____________________
55. ____________________
56. ____________________
57. ____________________
58. ____________________
59. ____________________
60. ____________________
61. ____________________
62. ____________________
63. ____________________
64. ____________________
65. ____________________
66. ____________________
67. ____________________
68. ____________________
69. ____________________
70. ____________________
71. ____________________
72. ____________________
73. ____________________
74. ____________________
75. ____________________
76. ____________________
77. ____________________
78. ____________________
79. ____________________
80. ____________________

81. ______________________________
82. ______________________________
83. ______________________________
84. ______________________________
85. ______________________________
86. ______________________________
87. ______________________________
88. ______________________________
89. ______________________________
90. ______________________________
91. ______________________________
92. ______________________________
93. ______________________________
94. ______________________________
95. ______________________________
96. ______________________________
97. ______________________________
98. ______________________________
99. ______________________________
100. ______________________________
101. ______________________________
102. ______________________________
103. ______________________________
104. ______________________________
105. ______________________________
106. ______________________________
107. ______________________________
108. ______________________________
109. ______________________________
110. ______________________________
111. ______________________________
112. ______________________________
113. ______________________________
114. ______________________________
115. ______________________________
116. ______________________________
117. ______________________________
118. ______________________________
119. ______________________________
120. ______________________________
121. ______________________________
122. ______________________________
123. ______________________________
124. ______________________________
125. ______________________________
126. ______________________________
127. ______________________________
128. ______________________________
129. ______________________________
130. ______________________________

131. ______________________

132. ______________________

133. ______________________

134. ______________________

135. ______________________

136. ______________________

137. ______________________

138. ______________________

139. ______________________

140. ______________________

141. ______________________

142. ______________________

143. ______________________

144. ______________________

145. ______________________

146. ______________________

147. ______________________

148. ______________________

149. ______________________

150. ______________________

PART B

Look at all you can do! But that's not all you are capable of. Draw up a list of all the things you are hesitant about doing but know you want to accomplish. Begin each thought by writing down the words, "I can."

SOUL RUBBING THREE:

You.
You Can.
You Can Risk.

Identify your fears then bid them goodbye. First, admit to them. Then follow this seven step process to help relinquish your top ten fears. It may take repetition to become fearless.

Example

1. I identify my fear of: (i.e. big dogs)

2. The worse case scenario if this fear is realized could be: (i.e. a big dog will attack me)

3. This fear holds me back from: (i.e. visiting my friend in her home as she has a big dog)

4. I think this fear comes from: (i.e. being jumped on by a big dog when I was a child)

5. I will confront this fear by: (i.e. making an appointment with a dog handler in order to get acquainted with big dogs in a safe way)

6. I will action #5 no later than: (i.e. date/time)

7. Releasing this fear has led to affirming action: (i.e. I now visit my friend's home and pat her dog)

Fear 1:

1. I identify my fear of:

___

2. The worse-case scenario if this fear is realized could be:

___

3. This fear holds me back from:

___

4. I think this fear comes from:

___

5. I will confront this fear by:

___

6. I will action #5 no later than:

___

7. Releasing this fear has led to affirmative action:

___

My Pot of Thoughts: ___

Fear 2:

1. I identify my fear of:

___

2. The worse-case scenario if this fear is realized could be:

___

3. This fear holds me back from:

___

4. I think this fear comes from:

___

5. I will confront this fear by:

___

6. I will action #5 no later than:

___

7. Releasing this fear has led to affirmative action:

___

My Pot of Thoughts: ___

Fear 3:

1. I identify my fear of:

2. The worse-case scenario if this fear could be:

3. This fear holds me back from:

4. I think this fear comes from:

5. I will confront this fear by:

6. I will action #5 no later than:

7. Releasing this fear has led to affirmative action:

My Pot of Thoughts:

Fear 4:

1. I identify my fear of:

____

2. The worse-case scenario if this fear is realized could be:

____

3. This fear holds me back from:

____

4. I think this fear comes from:

____

5. I will confront this fear by:

____

6. I will action #5 no later than:

____

7. Releasing this fear has led to affirmative action:

____

My Pot of Thoughts:

____

____

____

____

____

____

____

____

____

Fear 5:

1. I identify my fear of:

2. The worse-case scenario if this fear is realized could be:

3. This fear holds me back from:

4. I think this fear comes from:

5. I will confront this fear by:

6. I will action #5 no later than:

7. Releasing this fear has led to affirmative action:

My Pot of Thoughts:

Fear 6:

1. I identify my fear of:

2. The worse-case scenario if this fear is realized could be:

3. This fear holds me back from:

4. I think this fear comes from:

5. I will confront this fear by:

6. I will action #5 no later than:

7. Releasing this fear has led to affirmative action:

My Pot of Thoughts:

Fear 7:

1. I identify my fear of:

2. The worse-case scenario if this fear is realized could be:

3. This fear holds me back from:

4. I think this fear comes from:

5. I will confront this fear by:

6. I will action #5 no later than:

7. Releasing this fear has led to affirmative action:

My Pot of Thoughts:

Fear 8:

1. I identify my fear of:

2. The worse-case scenario if this fear is realized could be:

3. This fear holds me back from:

4. I think this fear comes from:

5. I will confront this fear by:

6. I will action #5 no later than:

7. Releasing this fear has led to affirmative action:

My Pot of Thoughts:

Fear 9:

1. I identify my fear of:

2. The worse-case scenario if this fear is realized could be:

3. This fear holds me back from:

4. I think this fear comes from:

5. I will confront this fear by:

6. I will action #5 no later than:

7. Releasing this fear has led to affirmative action:

My Pot of Thoughts:

Fear 10:

1. I identify my fear of:

2. The worse-case scenario if this fear is realized could be:

3. This fear holds me back from:

4. I think this fear comes from:

5. I will confront this fear by:

6. I will action #5 no later than:

7. Releasing this fear has led to affirmative action:

My Pot of Thoughts:

SOUL RUBBING FOUR:

You.
You Can.
You Can Risk.
You Can Risk Change.

PART A

This exercise was developed to help you identify any specific changes you need to make in your life. Make a check mark in the boxes following if they are true statements about you:

☐ I always tell the truth.

☐ I manipulate to get my way.

☐ I spread rumours.

☐ I am humble.

☐ I overwork.

☐ I always act kindly towards others.

☐ I always respect authority.

☐ I am very responsible with my finances.

☐ I purchase only what is needed.

☐ I speak of others in a derogatory manner.

☐ I run up my credit cards.

☐ I pay off my credit cards in full when the statement arrives.

☐ I repeat confidences.

☐ I always look at a situation carefully, understanding all points of view, before forming my own opinion.

☐ I always drive within the speed limit.

☐ I procrastinate.

☐ I am prompt for work or any appointments.

☐ I sometimes steal.

☐ I respect myself.

☐ I always eat to feed my mind and body in a healthy way.

☐ I exercise moderately.

☐ I have a good sense of humour.

☐ I am sarcastic.

☐ I am a control freak.

☐ I use food, drugs, or alcohol to make myself feel better.

☐ I am reckless.

☐ I take time to appreciate nature.

☐ I am compassionate.

☐ I am tolerant.

☐ I am good-hearted.

☐ I always think before I speak.

☐ I take responsibility for my mental health.

☐ I take responsibility for my physical health.

☐ I take responsibility for my spiritual health.

☐ I have healthy self-esteem.

☐ I understand my ego.

☐ I have my priorities straight.

☐ I am grateful.

☐ I am critical.

☐ I create crises in my life, or the lives of others.

☐ I am sometimes jealous.

☐ I am courageous.

☐ I always act with the best of intentions.

☐ I am vengeful.

☐ I make wise choices.

☐ I am impulsive.

☐ I give advise without being asked.

☐ I enable others to be irresponsible.

☐ I tithe.

☐ I am kind.

☐ I honour my body.

☐ I honour others.

☐ I honour Earth.

☐ I honour all living things.

☐ I honour my belongings.

☐ I honour the belongings of others.

☐ I give to those less fortunate.

☐ I am embarassed to face some people because of my past behaviour.

☐ I accept only what positively feeds my mind and body.

☐ I give and receive only that which fosters healthy relationships and that which is good for Earth, Sky, and Water.

My Pot of Thoughts:

___

___

___

___

PART B

Have you discovered aspects of your behaviour that you need to change? If so, please tell yourself about it by filling in the chart following:

Behaviour	Consequence	Change Required

Behaviour	Consequence	Change Required

SOUL RUBBING FIVE:

You.
You Can.
You Can Risk.
You Can Risk Change.
You Can Risk Change. Be Gentle.

PART A

Think about what you would describe as gentle. List these examples of gentleness in the spaces provided.

Example:

- A teardrop
- The inner membrane of an eggshell
- The tinkle of ice in a glass
- The purr of a kitten
- The sight of a fish jumping in the river

1. ______________________
2. ______________________
3. ______________________
4. ______________________
5. ______________________
6. ______________________
7. ______________________
8. ______________________
9. ______________________
10. ______________________
11. ______________________
12. ______________________
13. ______________________
14. ______________________
15. ______________________
16. ______________________
17. ______________________
18. ______________________
19. ______________________
20. ______________________
21. ______________________
22. ______________________
23. ______________________
24. ______________________

25. ______________________________
26. ______________________________
27. ______________________________
28. ______________________________
29. ______________________________
30. ______________________________
31. ______________________________
32. ______________________________
33. ______________________________
34. ______________________________
35. ______________________________
36. ______________________________
37. ______________________________
38. ______________________________
39. ______________________________
40. ______________________________
41. ______________________________
42. ______________________________
43. ______________________________
44. ______________________________
45. ______________________________
46. ______________________________
47. ______________________________
48. ______________________________
49. ______________________________
50. ______________________________
51. ______________________________
52. ______________________________
53. ______________________________
54. ______________________________
55. ______________________________
56. ______________________________
57. ______________________________
58. ______________________________
59. ______________________________
60. ______________________________
61. ______________________________
62. ______________________________
63. ______________________________
64. ______________________________
65. ______________________________
66. ______________________________
67. ______________________________
68. ______________________________
69. ______________________________
70. ______________________________
71. ______________________________
72. ______________________________
73. ______________________________
74. ______________________________

75. ____________________
76. ____________________
77. ____________________
78. ____________________
79. ____________________
80. ____________________
81. ____________________
82. ____________________
83. ____________________
84. ____________________
85. ____________________
86. ____________________
87. ____________________
88. ____________________
89. ____________________
90. ____________________
91. ____________________
92. ____________________
93. ____________________
94. ____________________
95. ____________________
96. ____________________
97. ____________________
98. ____________________
99. ____________________
100. ____________________
101. ____________________
102. ____________________
103. ____________________
104. ____________________
105. ____________________
106. ____________________
107. ____________________
108. ____________________
109. ____________________
110. ____________________
111. ____________________
112. ____________________
113. ____________________
114. ____________________
115. ____________________
116. ____________________
117. ____________________
118. ____________________
119. ____________________
120. ____________________
121. ____________________
122. ____________________
123. ____________________
124. ____________________

125. ______________________________

126. ______________________________

127. ______________________________

128. ______________________________

129. ______________________________

130. ______________________________

131. ______________________________

132. ______________________________

133. ______________________________

134. ______________________________

135. ______________________________

136. ______________________________

137. ______________________________

138. ______________________________

139. ______________________________

140. ______________________________

141. ______________________________

142. ______________________________

143. ______________________________

144. ______________________________

145. ______________________________

146. ______________________________

147. ______________________________

148. ______________________________

149. ______________________________

150. ______________________________

PART B

Please write letters to those you feel are mistreating you, or misunderstanding you, in some way. Do not send the letters but slip them under your mattress. Sleep on them. Dream on them.

My Pot of Thoughts:

PART C

Please write a letter to each of the individuals you identified in Part B, above. Write to each of them. State how you would like to be treated and/or understood. Slip those letters under your mattress. Sleep on them. Dream on them.

My Pot of Thoughts:

PART D

In your imagination, take the hand of one you remember, whom you loved and who has died. Ask that person's soul to assist you in identifying all the areas of your life that are harsh. Be open to accepting the fact that there may be areas of harshness in your relationships with family, friends, colleagues and strangers. Write a letter to yourself, and tell yourself what this loved one is saying to you. Place the letter under your mattress. Sleep on it. Dream on it.

My Pot of Thoughts:

SOUL RUBBING SIX:

You.
You Can.
You Can Risk.
You Can Risk Change.
You Can Risk Change. Be Gentle.
You Can Risk Change. Be Gentle. Be Giving.

PART A

Write about your patterns of giving – to yourself, and explain how these patterns make you feel. Define how these patterns affect your mind, your body, others and Earth.

PART B

Write about your patterns of giving – to others, and explain how these patterns make you feel. Define how these patterns affect your mind, your body, others and Earth.

PART C

Write about your patterns of receiving and how these patterns make you feel. Define what gifts you invite into your life. Define how these patterns of receiving affect your mind, your body, others and Earth.

PART D

Define any *imbalance in* your life. Outline how you are going to accomplish a new balance. Define how you think the personal balance you seek will affect your mind, your body, others and Earth.

SOUL RUBBING SEVEN:

You.
You Can.
You Can Risk.
You Can Risk Change.
You Can Risk Change. Be Gentle.
You Can Risk Change. Be Gentle. Be Giving.
You Can Risk Change. Be Gentle. Be Giving. Grow.

Draw on your feelings. Write a poem. Slash some colour on a canvas. Sing a song. Mold some clay. Take a photograph. Paddle through a marsh during high water. Walk a frozen river. Find a face in the clouds. Talk to the animals. Hold a baby. Find an open field and dance to a candle beneath the moon. Climb a hill and see the view from the top. Extend your open hand to one who needs help. Nurture Earth. Raise your arms to the heavens and invite love into your heart.

During a twenty eight day period, please state in ten words or less:

a) The highlight of your day.

b) Your perception of the day's highlight for a child subjected to poverty or abuse.

c) Your perception of a day's highlight for a child living in a war-torn area.

d) Your perception of a day's highlight for the planet on which we live.

Day One

a) ____________________

b) ____________________

c) ____________________

d) ____________________

Day Two

a) ____________________

b) ____________________

c) ____________________

d) ____________________

Day Three

a) ____________________

b) ____________________

c) ____________________

d) ____________________

Day Four

a) ____________________

b) ____________________

c) ____________________

d) ____________________

Day Five

a) ____________________

b) ____________________

c) ____________________

d) ____________________

Day Six

a) ____________________

b) ____________________

c) ____________________

d) ____________________

Day Seven

a) ____________________

b) ____________________

c) ____________________

d) ____________________

Day Eight

a) ______________________________

b) ______________________________

c) ______________________________

d) ______________________________

Day Nine

a) ______________________________

b) ______________________________

c) ______________________________

d) ______________________________

Day Ten

a) ______________________________

b) ______________________________

c) ______________________________

d) ______________________________

Day Eleven

a) ______________________________

b) ______________________________

c) ______________________________

d) ______________________________

Day Twelve

a) ______________________________

b) ______________________________

c) ______________________________

d) ______________________________

Day Thirteen

a) ______________________________

b) ______________________________

c) ______________________________

d) ______________________________

Day Fourteen

a) ______________________________

b) ______________________________

c) ______________________________

d) ______________________________

Day Fifteen

a) ______________________________

b) ______________________________

c) ______________________________

d) ______________________________

Day Sixteen

a) ______________________________

b) ______________________________

c) ______________________________

d) ______________________________

Day Seventeen

a) ______________________________

b) ______________________________

c) ______________________________

d) ______________________________

Day Eighteen

a) ______

b) ______

c) ______

d) ______

Day Nineteen

a) ______

b) ______

c) ______

d) ______

Day Twenty

a) ______

b) ______

c) ______

d) ______

Day Twenty-one

a) ______

b) ______

c) ______

d) ______

Day Twenty-two

a) ______

b) ______

c) ______

d) ______

Day Twenty-three

a) ______________________________

b) ______________________________

c) ______________________________

d) ______________________________

Day Twenty-four

a) ______________________________

b) ______________________________

c) ______________________________

d) ______________________________

Day Twenty-five

a) ______________________________

b) ______________________________

c) ______________________________

d) ______________________________

Day Twenty-six

a) ______________________________

b) ______________________________

c) ______________________________

d) ______________________________

Day Twenty-seven

a) ______________________________

b) ______________________________

c) ______________________________

d) ______________________________

Day Twenty-eight

a) ______

b) ______

c) ______

d) ______

My Pot of Thoughts: ______

SOUL RUBBING EIGHT

You.
You Can.
You Can Risk.
You Can Risk Change.
You Can Risk Change. Be Gentle.
You Can Risk Change. Be Gentle. Be Giving.
You Can Risk Change. Be Gentle. Be Giving. Grow.
You Can Risk Change. Be Gentle. Be Giving. Grow. Pass It On.

I now ask you to consider what you have learned about yourself.

PART A

I believe (or do not believe) we are the sum of our thoughts.

My Pot of Thoughts:______________________________

____

____

____

____

____

PART B

I will (or will not) begin each day, conscious of my thoughts.

My Pot of Thoughts:______________________________

____

____

____

____

____

____

PART C

I will take what I have learned about myself and am prepared to pass on my soul gifts to others.

My Pot of Thoughts:

PART D: CALL TO ACTION

I am prepared to lead a circle. This circle will focus on the giving and receiving of soul gifts. I envision the evolvement of this circle in a creative way and define its creation in my Pot of Thoughts.

My Pot of Thoughts:

Soul Gifts: The World's Self-Help Book

— a breakthrough in personal and collective evolvement.

by

Barbara J Gill, R.N.

This is a book for women and for men who are not afraid to connect to that vulnerable place of soul. It is a book to talk about over coffee, to share with partners, mates, friends and family. It is also a book to ponder in quiet moments. And it is, the author hopes, a stimulus to action.

Barbara takes us lovingly through vignettes of her life experiences - interwoven with poems, paintings, song and people – to lead us gently to her philosophy for living: "You. You can. You can risk" . . . Barbara's very human experiences will inspire you and instill the confidence you need to make changes in your life.

Harry Gill figures in the narrative through his letters home. He was Barbara's father's brother. He joined the RCAF at the outbreak of WWII, became a fighter pilot, somehow transferred to the RAF, saw the UK, South Africa, and India. He was shot down by a Zero over India in 1943. He was twenty years old when he died. He is buried in Bangladesh.

Barbara's poems are short, clear and to the point. They relate, in memorable expressions, the themes of the chapters. Readers will find themselves quoting from these verses.

The "Voices Within" becomes the string of the book calling us to join in thought and theme. Not just the author's voice is heard. Old friends speak, family, people Barbara has met over the years, people she has worked with, children, the very old, homebodies, people who live large, people the reader will like to know – from Aunt Florence to a tidal wave surfer in California.

Soul Gifts advocates change, growth, improvement, but "One day at a time.". . . nothing drastic. But do it. Improve you. You can. Improve your life. You will. Improve this beautiful world. That will follow automatically. *This book speaks of the "Human Chain" - how we are all connected and how we can use this connection for peace and prosperity, not by organizing for the "the cause" but by living it. You. You can. You will . . .*

For more information about this book and Barbara J. Gill, RN, please visit; www.shandarrah.com.

ISBN 978-1-4116-9045-5

About the Author

Barbara J Gill, a registered nurse by profession, is a writer and visual artist who brings a practical approach to her teachings. Her service-oriented background, political and labour activism, and career as a businesswoman are evidence of her versatility. Barbara has written for half a century; she has her first poem from 1956 and her journals date back to the age of ten.

A former psychiatric and palliative care nurse, "B J" – as some call her – returned to the profession in 2001. She now works part-time in an extended care facility. She is the mother to three and a grandmother to one.

Author Contact:

Barbara J. Gill, RN
PO Box 3397, Fredericton,
New Brunswick, Canada,
E3A 5H2
www.shandarrah.com

www.ingramcontent.com/pod-product-compliance
Ingram Content Group UK Ltd.
Pitfield, Milton Keynes, MK11 3LW, UK
UKHW041927190726
13854UKWH00003B/1486

9 781411 690455